ROTHERHAM
THEN & NOW

MARGARET DRINKALL

AND CHRIS DRINKALL

First published 2012

The History Press
The Mill, Brimscombe Port
Stroud, Gloucestershire, GL5 2QG
www.thehistorypress.co.uk

ISBN 978 0 7524 6545 6

Typesetting and origination by The History Press
Printed in India

CONTENTS

ACKNOWLEDGEMENTS

It almost goes without saying that this book could not have been written without the encouragement of The History Press; I would like to particularly thank Jennifer Briancourt for her excellent editing. I also owe a debt of gratitude to the staff of the Rotherham Archives and Local Studies Department, notably Chris Evans, one of the Local Studies librarians who put her own massive workload on hold in order to help me out with the illustrations for the book. All the old photographs are courtesy of the Rotherham Archives and Local Studies collection, and can be viewed in the Local Studies department on the Viewfinder. I must also extend my grateful thanks to my son Chris, who has taken the modern-day photographs for the book.

Margaret Drinkall
July 2012

I'd like to thank my family and friends, who have supported (put up with) me over the years; my co-author mother (she's a great person and loves history, as you can probably tell from the local history sections in your nearby bookshops); my brother Steve; my gorgeous partner Sally; my dad; and my university pals: Monkey, Josh Phillips, John Ball, Andy Wilson, Nick Woods, Dom, Steven Jones, Thomas Atkinson.

Chris Drinkall
July 2012

INTRODUCTION

This book is an attempt to uncover little-known facts about the places and areas of interest that we have in Rotherham. Most people know the history behind our famous landmarks and streets, but this book is an attempt to show you a different side of things. I have included some old historic buildings that have been covered in local history books before and have also added modern, functional, civic buildings of interest. A comparison of the 'then' and 'now' photographs illustrates that, while some places have changed for the better, many more have changed for the worse. But this book is intended to be honest and unbiased – 'warts and all', if you will.

Rotherham has long held a significant place in the history of the North of England. As we all know, it was visited by Mary Queen of Scots as well as Charles I. Herbert Wroe tells us that, in 1536, the town was the base for the army of King Henry VIII during the uprising known as the Pilgrimage of Grace. We know that by 1750 Rotherham was still mainly rural, with the majority of houses clustered around the main streets of the town. These were Wellgate, High Street, Westgate, College Street and Bridgegate. Many of these early roads would have had gates or 'yates' on them, hence the names, but beyond these roads lay nothing but fields.

Many excellent books have already been written about Rotherham and its past, which I have listed in the bibliography. I admit that, combined with the newspapers of the period, I have dug deep into these books in order to extract different facts. However, I have to say that any mistakes in the book are my own and if they are pointed out to me they will be rectified in the next book. I hope that, between these pages, you the reader will find some information that you didn't know about the familiar places of Rotherham.

ALL SAINTS SQUARE

ALL SAINTS SQUARE has long been one of the most historic squares of the town; a place where people would congregate. Situated in front of the Rotherham Minster, it has been used as a meeting place for centuries, ever since the days of the College of Jesus in the fifteenth century. It has been the site of one of the earlier courthouses, and Rotherham's first dispensary, library and reading rooms. It is also thought to be the place where the ancient stocks were kept to punish local felons. In 1930, it was decided by the town council that major alterations would be made to All Saints Square in order to create a new transport centre. These alterations would involve the disturbance and removal of

ALL SAINTS SQUARE, RO

some of the graves within the churchyard. Permission was sought from the church authorities, and the bodies were re-interred in a service led by Revd Canon Morgan, the vicar of the Minster (then regarded as the parish church). The introduction of motor buses in 1913 supplemented the tram and trolley bus (known as trackless) service which was already running in Rotherham.

The new transport centre was opened on Monday, 20 March 1933. What is less known is that somewhere under the present square is the site of underground toilets, built in the 1930s, which were made of reinforced concrete and white-glazed bricks. Situated in the centre of the town, the bus station continued until January 1967, when the new Transport Interchange was built. Understandably, the square has seen many celebrations – such as the one on Sunday, 15 November 1942, when the Minster bells pealed out to celebrate the success of the 8th Army in Egypt. Church bells had been banned throughout the war years and it had been agreed that they would only be rung if an invasion had taken place. Such was the country's delight at their victory, that the ban was temporarily lifted. A civic parade was held by the new Mayor, Alderman J. Dickinson, who walked from the Town Hall to the Minster to hear a service of thanksgiving. This was followed by a salute from members of the civil defence units. In May 1944, there was a demonstration of Ack-Ack guns held in the square, as well as a parade of the Home Guard. But there is little doubt that the greatest celebrations were held at the end of the Second World War.

THE BLUECOAT SCHOOL

IN A MEETING of the town trustees, which are known in Rotherham as the Feoffees of the Common Lands, held on 2 January 1775, it was agreed that a new charity school for poor children be opened in the town. By 22 June, plans were in place to purchase a piece of land situated on the site of the old beast market on the Crofts. At a later meeting, which took place on 16 August 1775, it was agreed that the clothing of the children attending the charity school would be:

Blue jackets with a single row of buttons, a red collar and cuffs of two inches wide. Breeches to be made high on the hip to come down to the middle of the calf, without knee buttons. The caps, blue with small red front. The dress of the girls shall be blue serge with narrow red cuffs, linen capes and tippets, grey yarn stockings for the boys and blue for the girls. The whole of this to be put on new every Whit Sunday.

Inevitably, because of the dress, the school became known as the Bluecoat School when it opened in 1776. It was said that the school was a favourite project of the Feoffees, as they assiduously searched the records in order to establish that only the poorest and most deserving of working-class children were admitted with a scholarship. By 1779, the Feoffees' accounts show that the school had forty-eight children, and, by the 1850s, the numbers had risen to forty boys and thirty girls. It was said that one of the masters was a man named John Clarke who, although only having one hand, could 'wield the cane vigorously'. Pupils who misbehaved would be dealt with summarily. The girls would be sent out of the school whilst the culprit, mounted on another boy, would be thrashed soundly. In his book, George Gummer conveys his memories of the 1860s, when the charity boys of the Bluecoat School wore their distinctive dress, which inevitably would set them apart from other boys of the town. Thankfully, the uniform was later abandoned.

The charity school closed its doors in 1892 but the building was taken over by other groups, such as in 1905 when it became the Young Men's Christian Institute. In 1912, the building housed the Labour Institute. Even later still, it became a confectionary warehouse, a private residence, a dancing academy, a garage and a baker's workshop. The building has since turned into a very popular public house.

BOROUGH POLICE COURT AND OFFICES, FREDERICK STREET

IT WAS AGREED by the town council in 1895 that a new police court was required, and so a site was found on Frederick Street. The designated site consisted of a series of buildings, and one of them had been a music hall run by a man named Charlie Gill; in 1876, the hall had passed into the possession of the Temperance Society. The whole block was emptied of former tenants and a large section was

turned into the police station and magistrates' court, which was opened to great acclaim on 27 July 1895. A reporter from the local newspaper described the building, which was mainly made of red brick with stone-dressed edges:

The public entrance led to both courts and the magistrates' rooms are magnificent in their construction. Waiting rooms are accessed by a central stone staircase which is approximately five feet wide. The remainder of the frontage of the building is taken up with the police offices. There is a large hall and lobby leading directly into the charge room and the Chief Inspector office. The lobby also gives access to the Chief Constable's office where a strong room can be found. There is also a large parade room as well as a private entrance to the Chief Inspector's house on the first floor. His accommodation consists of, living room, kitchens, scullery and bedrooms.

He proudly reported that inside the new police station there were fifteen cells, and each cell was well ventilated and lit. The cells contained a water closet and a bench for the comfort of the prisoners. The corridor leading to the cells was also described as being very well lit and decorated with white-glazed bricks. As could be expected, the entrance from the cells to the docks was kept entirely separate from the public part of the building. The first-floor offices had 'rooms for barristers, client consultation rooms, separate witness rooms, magistrates' clerks' offices and store rooms'. The building still exists today, although it is no longer a police station and magistrates' court, as they have now moved to Main Street. This triangular-shape structure, which borders Howard Street and Effingham Street, also holds the Old Town Hall. Although parts of it are empty at the present moment in time, this magnificent building once reflected great civic pride.

BOSTON CASTLE AND PARK

BOSTON CASTLE HAD initially started life as a shooting lodge for the 3rd Earl of Effingham, Thomas Howard. By March 1774, the interior was described as having a passage and two little chambers, the best chamber being equipped with a fireplace. There was also a cellar with a stone table. But it was only when the building was completed that the folly got its name – from the infamous Boston Tea Party, which had taken place in December 1773. As a result of the Boston Tea Party, George III had brought in the Coercive Acts, which reduced the powers of self-government for the colonists. There was much protest about this in Britain, and Thomas Howard resigned his

commission rather than fight against the American people. He also declared that tea was banned in his new folly and the name Boston Castle was born. In May 1873, the town council decided to purchase the castle and grounds from the 7th Earl of Effingham, for the use of the people of Rotherham. He kindly granted a forty-year lease for an annual rent of £50. To great celebrations, the castle and the park were opened to the public on 4 July 1876, which also coincided with the American Declaration of Independence. The event started with the Rotherham Volunteer Brass Band marching through the town on their way to the new grounds, to tumultuous cheers and waving of flags. Thousands of visitors came to the park and, in the evening, the Westgate railway station was reported as being 'thronged with people returning home'. Having such vast open spaces, the park became the venue for many local events, which were held frequently over the years. On one such occasion, the entertainment provided included such innocent acts as acrobats, comic singers and dancers. However, this was deemed 'not to be appropriate', and the disapproving town council decided against such a repetition. The castle was put to more practical use during the Second World War, when it was used as a lookout from its vantage point overlooking the town. Sadly, during the 1960s, the castle and park once again became neglected but it was not until 1975 that the Rotherham Council decided to give the whole park a facelift. The opening of the new park was a two-day event, starting on 4 July 1976, when both British and American flags were seen over the castle. In order for as many people of the town to enjoy the park and castle, a free bus service was laid on from the centre of the town. Boston Castle and parklands are once again experiencing a massive refurbishment, which is expected to finish in 2012 so that the people of Rotherham can continue to enjoy this historic local landmark.

BRIDGEGATE

DURING THE CIVIL War, the town was attacked by the Royalist Earl of Newcastle, and, despite a brave attempt, the people of Rotherham had to surrender due to a lack of ammunition. A promise had been made that, if the town surrendered, no looting would take place – but, as soon as the army gained entrance, many buildings were set on fire. It was reported that the Earl triumphantly

raced up Bridgegate, where he gave orders that prominent citizens of the town were to be rounded up. Several of these men were imprisoned in the Chapel on the Bridge, and were fined 1,000 marks each. Bridgegate then, as you can see from the photograph, was a much narrower street that became a bottleneck in times of stormy weather. Gummer tells us that, after the Dale Dyke dam burst at Sheffield on Friday, 11 March 1864, the water rose steadily up Bridgegate. Thankfully, the inhabitants had been warned and managed to get to higher ground. It was reported that, within minutes, the water level had reached the cellars of two eating houses on the same spot as where the New County Hotel and the Angel Inn stand today. Several dead bodies were recovered from the bottom of Bridgegate, 'many of them respectably dressed'. One of the most pitiful sights was that of a baby in a cradle, which fortunately was rescued alive further down the river. Gummer also remembers a time when Bridgegate was a more pastoral place, where people would meet.
He says that at the bottom of Bridgegate they would be able to take a pleasant walk along the banks of the river, where 'only a few old cottages stood'. Despite the romantic country scene, the local newspaper of February 1863 suggested that there was a good reason why the soubriquet 'dirty Rotherham' still held ground:

> To rival our dirty streets, smoky atmosphere and earthy water ... A slow muddy stream so thick and deep as that which flows undisturbed in wet weather is seen going through Bridgegate and on towards the railway.

In a letter written to the *Advertiser* on 12 April 1890, a resident of the town remembers that he witnessed the last public thrashing, which had taken place sixty years earlier. He said that the man, who had been a thief, was tied to a cart in Bridgegate and thrashed all the way along College Street, along the High Street, and the bottom of Westgate before being released. As can be seen by the present-day photograph, many of the old buildings of Bridgegate were demolished and the road was widened in the 1900s.

BRIDGE INN

THERE HAS BEEN a Bridge Inn in the town since 1778 and there have been many landlords of character during that time. It seems that a former landlord of the old Bridge Inn was an adventurer called Captain George Ridgeway, who had been taken prisoner by the French during the Napoleonic Wars. Eventually, his career ended and he settled down to spend the rest of his days in the town. His body was finally buried in Rotherham churchyard, where his tombstone read:

Captain George Ridgeway of the Bridge Inn Masbrough
who departed from this life July 12th 1847 aged 58 years

Rotherham was a town which had more than its fair share of pubs, beerhouses and inns. Consequently, drunkenness was very common. It was also legal practice to hold inquests at the nearest public house to where a corpse was found. In January 1863, the coroner Mr J. Webster held an inquest at the Bridge Inn on a labouring man, James Biscombe, whose body had been found in the River Don; a witness told the coroner that he was 'a very drunken man who spent most of his wages in drink'. The coroner suggested that Biscombe had been making his way home by the canal side when his foot had slipped and he had fallen in the water and drowned; a verdict of accidental death was duly recorded. In the 1850s, men who were discovered to be drunk were put in the stocks near to the church, and remained there until noon in order to ensure maximum humiliation. It was said that in many cases the treatment was effective, as the offence was not repeated. The original Bridge Inn was knocked down and the present Bridge Inn (seen in both photographs) built nearby. Many famous people have reportedly passed through its doors. A letter written by Stan Crowther, the president of CAMRA, was sent to the *Rotherham Advertiser* in October 1995, commiserating on the fact that the inn was once more to close. He reminisced about the skiffle groups that were held there in the 1950s. He remembered comedian Duggie Brown from Maltby, who would often turn up with his guitar for a jamming session only to find that he could make people laugh instead. Thankfully, the present Bridge Inn (also known as Nellie Dean's) continues to thrive and is a popular meeting place for Rotherham people today.

CATTLE MARKET

THE CATTLE MARKET was held on the Crofts for many years and is one of the highest spots of the town. Markets had been held in Rotherham since the monks of Rufford Abbey were granted a licence in 1316. At one time, it was said to be one of the largest cattle markets in the North of England. Every Monday, a market was held where beasts were bought and sold, and it was so popular that stalls would frequently spill over into Mansfield Road. On market day, it was reported that crowds of visitors on horsebacks and in conveyances would descend on the town. Every Whit Monday, a horse fair was held, which again was so well attended that buyers and sellers could be seen a fair distance up Moorgate Road. Gummer describes it as being very hard to get through the crowds that attended

these horse fairs; they did a roaring trade. As well as being a cattle market, however, this was also a place of entertainment. When King Edward married Princess Alexandra on 10 March 1863, fireworks were let off at the cattle market in the evening where (due to its high position) they would have been seen all over the town. The Yorkshire Dragoons would assemble there before their annual fortnight-long camp at Doncaster, and hundreds of people would come to see them off. As many of the horses were on loan from the farmers of the district, they would often turn up to see their own beasts. The Dragoons were usually accompanied by a band, guaranteeing that a good number of people would turn out to wave them off. On a darker note, it was recorded that after the election riots of 1852, the Riot Act was read to a mob that had collected on the cattle market. The Hussars attacked the fleeing crowd and people used the wooden rails of the pens to defend themselves from the sabre-rattling militia. In July 1898, the sanitary committee received a complaint that effluent from the cattle was running down Ship Hill and Corporation Street, and collecting in a children's playground. Rain did not improve the problem as it would combine with the blood, urine and faeces on the same journey before ending up in the canal. The local newspaper complained that 'the practice had become a perfect nuisance' and demanded that 'it was high time the Corporation dealt with it'. The same year, it was decided that the Town Hall would be built on the Crofts, and the cattle market was removed.

THE CENOTAPH

IN FEBRUARY 1921, plans went ahead to build a cenotaph in Rotherham which would list all the names of the men who had died in the First World War. The word cenotaph means 'empty grave', and it seemed an appropriate memorial to the thousands of Rotherham men who had lost their lives and were buried in foreign lands. It was anticipated that the unveiling ceremony would be attended by the Prince of Wales (later the Duke of Windsor). However, due to illness, the Prince had to cancel and the ceremony went ahead on 26 November 1922, attended by Lt-Gen Sir Ivor Maxse. The tablets behind the cenotaph hold the names of 1,304 men who died in the war, but there is no room to record the stories of the bravery of these young men. For example, one of the names is that

of Private Arthur Shadlock, who was killed in action on 28 March 1915. He had signed up at the commencement of the war and had gone to France on 1 Nov 1914. The last letter his mother received from him was a week earlier, dated 21 March, when he told her that he was 'cheerful and well'. Another soldier whose name is on the memorial is Private Harry Willett, who had spent only three weeks in the trenches before being killed in action near Ypres in April 1915. He was only thirty years of age and had been born in College Street in Rotherham. The commanding officer of his company sent a letter to his parents, stating that although he had not been very long with the company, he had 'already shown himself to be a brave and cheerful soldier'. He went on to inform the family that Private Willett was shot in the trenches in the evening and had consequently died at the dressing station a few hours later without regaining consciousness. The deceased soldier had been buried in a small enclosure with some of his comrades 'in a small wood outside Ypres'. Also recorded is the death of Rifleman S. Mace, who was killed in action at Neuve Chapelle on 12 March 1915. This soldier was only twenty-eight years of age and he left a wife and a child for whom much sympathy was felt. These three men are examples of the brave soldiers of Rotherham who are remembered every year on Armistice Day, when wreaths are placed for them on Rotherham Cenotaph.

CHAPEL ON THE BRIDGE

THE HISTORIC CHAPEL on the Bridge is laid on the site of an ancient paved footway which stretched across the river for travellers entering the town. The bridge and the chapel were built by Thomas Rotherham during the years 1481–3, but in 1547, when chantry lands were disposed of, the chapel became a prison and later a tobacconist shop, before being re-consecrated as a chapel once more on 22 July 1924. George Gummer tells us that in the 1850s it was a regular sight to see prisoners calling out to passers-by through the bars of their cells, asking friends to bring them some tobacco. The cell is still in the chapel and can be seen on open days. Gummer also states that a fire was lit on the Masbrough side every year, and a man demanded a toll for each head of cattle or sheep that passed over, although there is no indication of who this man was or his authority to collect tolls. In 1858, the prison was converted into a dwelling house; the records of the Feoffees indicate that, 'Mr Bland be given notice to quit and Mr Jas Handley to be the new tenant at £7 p.a'. Guest, in his *Relics and Records*, tells us that a ducking pool was situated under the first arch of the bridge

(at present under the Transport Exchange). This pool, which was said to be a deep one, was used to 'duck' scolds or gossips. He reports that husbands would sometimes pay 1s 6d for their wives to be ducked for that purpose. These poor women were lowered into the water sitting in a heavy chair, which was suspended by iron rings. We know that the chair was in use until as late as 1632. There are four reports of women being ducked in this fashion in the Feoffees' accounts of 1579, 1592, 1611 and 1632. They also recorded two dates when the ducking chair was washed away by floods. When the new road was added alongside the Chantry Bridge, Herbert Morrison was invited to open the road on Monday, 28 April 1930. Councillor Dickenson told the crowd that Cardinal Wolsey had passed over the bridge on 9 November 1529 on his fateful journey to Leicester, where he died twenty days later. Today, the Chapel on the Bridge is one of the oldest monuments we have in Rotherham, and is the only one of three such chapels still in existence in Britain today.

CHURCH STREET

AS CAN BE imagined, Church Street runs down the side of the Minster church. Therefore it might surprise people to know that in 1857 there were two public houses opposite the Minster. The old Ring O'Bells had been established for many years at No.8, and at that time was run by Mary Anne Jackson. Next door at No.6 was the White Hart, run by Henry Smith. Some people may question the necessity of having two public houses so near to the church but William Blazeby felt that, on the contrary, the association between church and inn was very close – this was due to people travelling from outlying areas around the town in order to attend ceremonies at the church. It may also have been due to the fact that the vicar and churchwardens received 20s a year for the

church tithes from the owners of the Ring O'Bells, as stated when the pub was put up for sale on 12 February 1933. We know there was a long history of pubs on Church Street. In 1642, King Charles I had fled to York, where he demanded support from all his subjects north of the River Trent. His troops demanded that the town of Rotherham supply:

...money, plate, arms or horses for the loan of which 8 per cent is offered. Those that are able to provide any are to meet at the Inn on Church Street at the house of Widow Clayton.

The order threatens 'fail at your peril'. Herbert Wroe suggests that Widow Clayton could have been the wife of William Clayton, who had been a landlord of an unnamed inn in 1627. He further suggests that she was the possible mother of Luke Clayton, who was appointed Vicar of Rotherham in 1644–62. In *Reminiscences of Rotherham* (a series of letters in the *Rotherham Advertiser* which were later made into a book), one letter writer speaks of vivid childhood memories of seeing bodies of cholera victims being carried down Church Street in baskets. The churchyard had been closed for burials as it was feared that re-opening graves would spread the contagion, and the bodies were eventually buried on some land on Doncaster Road. Today, little remains of the busy shops trading in the old photograph (which was taken in 1936); indeed, only the Imperial Buildings can be seen today. Where the workmen fences are placed is where Rotherham Council is building a pleasant garden and seating area, which will be known as Minster Yard. Sadly, that is all that is left of such a historic site today.

CIVIC BUILDING

EVERY TOWN HAS to have administration buildings which were built for their functionality rather than designed as a thing of beauty. The area which today is occupied by the Civic Building and the library was bulldozed to the ground in the late 1960s to provide a centre of administration. The building was opened in August 1974 and is typical of the municipal buildings of the period, built of concrete and steel. When it was opened, it was criticized as 'brutalist', with some claiming that it looked like something from the Czech Republic. The Civic Building was further criticized in November 1993 for being built the wrong way round. The entrance overlooked the car park, and the double doors leading from Walker Place were said to be unsafe. At the time, there had been two

recent accidents when members of the public had slipped on the steps leading into the building. There were claims that only one of the double doors could be opened. The interior was criticized for having inadequate interview space and cramped waiting areas. Worst of all for the people paying rates and enquiring about housing benefits, there was only one toilet. The idea of the provision of better customer service centres was mooted in 2003 and the Civic Building was seen as a flagship for others. Two years later, in July 2005, the building was newly refurbished to provide a customer-friendly service to people entering the building. The reception was designed to be open plan, and therefore gives light and space to the once cramped rooms. The building incorporates the Rotherham ideal of a 'one-stop shop', where people of the town can find access to many local services. Plans are now in place for a new Civic Building to be built as part of the Rotherham Renaissance on the site of the old Guest & Chrimes building on the Don Street/Main Street site. A design has been approved by architects Carey Jones and the building is expected to be completed shortly. The new building will be called Riverside House and will incorporate the new library service, which is its present neighbour on Walker Place.

CLIFTON MUSEUM

CLIFTON HOUSE, A Grade II listed building, is now a museum for the people of the town. The house first came on the market when the man who had it built in the 1780s, Henry Walker, died in 1860. The house was then sold to William Owen Esq., who was the owner of the Phoenix Iron Works. Following his death in 1881, the house was occupied by Mr Charles H. Thornhill Esq., who put the house and gardens on the market in February 1883. The contents up for sale and the list of furniture from the house were described in the *Rotherham Advertiser*, which gives us an insight into the type of furnishing found in the house of a wealthy Victorian family. The advertisement states that the mansion house included an entrance hall, breakfast room, conservatory, kitchen and

laundry rooms. Upstairs there were seven good-sized bedrooms, one of which had a dressing room attached. In the lower part of the house was a well-stocked wine cellar, containing 150 dozen bottles of fine old wine, including port and vintage sherries advertised to be in 'first class condition'. The house contents included large amounts of mahogany furniture from the bedrooms and dining room, a full-size billiard table and 'cottage pianofortes'. Also included was a bronze metal umbrella stand, as well as engravings 'after the style of Edwin Landseer'. Several valuable oil paintings were offered by such artists as Sir Peter Lely, William Thomas Hawksworth and others. Additionally for sale were a 'small collection of china including specimens of old Crown Derby and Rockingham'. In the yard and outbuildings there were various farming implements, as well as a two-horse brougham, a splendid bath chair, a stove and greenhouse plants. The other buildings attached to Clifton House which no longer exist included a gardener's house, a stable with two stalls, harness rooms, a carriage house and piggeries. The kitchen garden contained vineries, a potting shed and a cucumber house. A week before the advertisement of the sale, a letter had appeared in the paper asking the town council to buy the house and parkland for the people of the town. Despite the wishes of the ratepayers, the house and park were not bought by the Corporation until June 1891 at a cost of £25,000, and two years later the house became a museum, which still opens it doors to visitors today. Designed to be a 'hands on' experience of history, the museum attracts hundreds of visitors each year.

CLIFTON PARK

THE GATES OF Clifton Park over the centuries have seen millions of people entering to enjoy the tranquillity and beauty of its scenery. The history of the area goes back a long time, before even Clifton House was built. We know that during the Civil War in 1643, cannons were placed on the site where the museum is now and were fired on the Royalists who were attacking the people of the town. We also know that there were gallows erected somewhere in the same area, overlooking the town. But generally speaking, the park has long been used for the pleasure of its townspeople. The park was formally opened by the Prince of Wales in June 1891, where vast crowds were being entertained by all kinds of festivities. The principal attraction was a balloon ascent, with the balloon being filled with gas from the town's mains. At the start of the ascent, one of the town's councillors had a narrow escape as his legs became entangled with the rope, but, fortunately, he

managed to free himself. In the evening, the whole affair was rounded off by a grand firework display. The size of the park ensured that an immense crowd gathered to welcome home the eight soldiers who had been fighting in the Boer War in June 1901. Factories and workshops were closed for the day to allow as many people as possible to join in with the celebration and, as a result, it was recorded that the park was 'packed with people'. The men marched into the park accompanied by the Corporation Officers and the church choristers in their white surplices. The band played 'Home Sweet Home' and 'Soldiers of the King' to glorious applause and waving of union jacks.

As a stark contrast to these joyous scenes, the park was bombed in 1942 when a German bomber saw the tents erected for the 'Holidays at Home' scheme and assumed that it was an army camp. Generally, the park was used for joyful occasions, such as for part of the same scheme in August 1942, when Fossett's Circus was in the park exhibiting no fewer than '50 animals including monkeys, tigers, bears and lions'. Thanks to a grant of £4.5m from the Heritage Lottery Fund, the park continues to evolve as a place of beauty and entertainment for the people of the town.

COLLEGE SQUARE

COLLEGE SQUARE IS barely recognisable today, although one building (which has EMPIRE written down the side wall in the old image) still remains the same. Like other places in Rotherham, the square was a regular meeting and assembly place. When men were leaving the town for York to train for what was to become known as the Boer War, large numbers came out to give them a 'hearty send off'. It was also the scene of great rejoicing on the evening of Friday, 19 May 1900, when news reached the town that Mafeking had been relieved. George Gummer, who was the Mayor of the town, gave a speech in College Square and it was reported that the bells of the Minster mingled with the cheers of the people. Long after midnight, the revellers paraded through the town. On another occasion, the square played host to the scene of a horrific death. The police force in Rotherham began in April 1882 and in that same year the first chief constable appointed was a

man called John Pollard – a very popular choice. He died six years after his appointment, at the age of forty-one, crossing College Square to attend to a fire. The *Rotherham Advertiser* described him, on 4 July 1888, as:

A man who had been rigidly impartial and just in his public life as well as his private life. He leaned neither to the left nor the right. Although small in stature being only five foot five inches, he had an excellent command of the police force and fully merited his appointment. Bright and cheery his courtesy and prepossessing manner won him many friends. His death took place with startling suddenness, under painful circumstances and in the prime of his life.

The political unrest of the years of 1919 and 1920 saw the square being used for speeches as local communists spread their literature. On several occasions, it was reported that the square had been 'taken over by the advocates of Lenin and Trotsky'. When it was announced that the visit of Princess Mary would take place on 7 September 1925, concerns were expressed for her safety because of the communists in the town. The chief constable later thanked his officers for 'the efficient manner in which they dealt with the communist meeting in College Square thus preventing any suggestion of unpleasantness being brought to the notice of the Royal Visitor'.

CORONATION BRIDGE

CORONATION BRIDGE CAME into being because of the introduction of trams to the Kimberworth route. Prior to that, traffic to Kimberworth and Masbrough had gone under the railway through a very little bridge; great care had to be taken due to its narrowness. When people complained that traffic was being held up by carts and carriages having to queue up to pass under the bridge, the town council knew that something must be done. More traffic was going to travel through Masbrough and Kimberworth with the opening of the railway station, so it was deemed necessary for action to be taken. At first, the railway company applied for a Bill to widen the road which passed under the bridge, but it was opposed 'might and main by the Corporation'. Eventually, it was agreed

that a new bridge was to be built over the railway. The bridge was opened by the Mayoress, Mrs Jenkinson, on Wednesday, 8 April 1903 and named after the Coronation of Edward VII. The opening ceremony took place on a bright, sunny day and many of the townspeople arrived by tram from the Assembly Rooms in the town. The Mayoress opened the bridge for vehicular transport to rousing cheers. After passing over the bridge in a landau, the party went to the Prince of Wales Hotel for light refreshments. Congratulatory speeches were made after the refreshments had been served. Alderman Winter thanked the Mayoress and added that, although it was not the most beautiful of bridges, it was the most substantial bridge he had seen. Alderman Hickmott congratulated the council on their success of the tramway system and stated that, 'if the trams pay their way from the beginning it will be a great success'.

Today, if pedestrians study the walls along both sides of Coronation Bridge, evidence can be seen of the bricking-up of wooden steps. There were originally two sets of wooden stairs leading from the bridge down to Holmes Lane. At the other end of the bridge, one can see evidence of steps down to Masbrough Station itself. Although the trams have long gone, the bridge remains essential today for the route towards not only Kimberworth, but Ferham, Holmes and Meadowhall Shopping Centre, which receives over twenty-five million people a year.

DONCASTER GATE

DONCASTER GATE WAS one of the main entry roads into the town and was originally the site of two windmills, although nothing remains of them today. During the Civil War in January 1643, it was recorded that the Royalists who had attacked the town were forced to retreat up Doncaster Gate with their dead and wounded. It was also the road which started off the ancient ceremony known as 'the Beating of the Bounds'. Crowds of people joined in this ceremony, which went from Doncaster Gate to Dalton Brook through Bramley, Wickersley, Brecks and Whiston. In the 1840s, the bellman or town crier was a man named Dick Davison, and he would take a horse and cart loaded with two barrels of beer and some bread, cheese and ginger bread nuts for the people

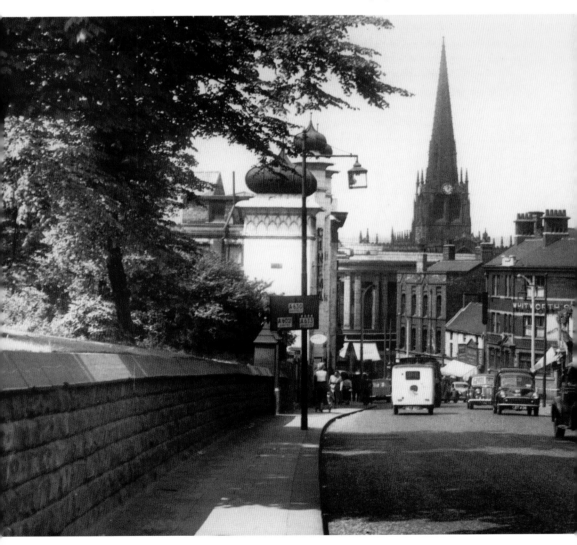

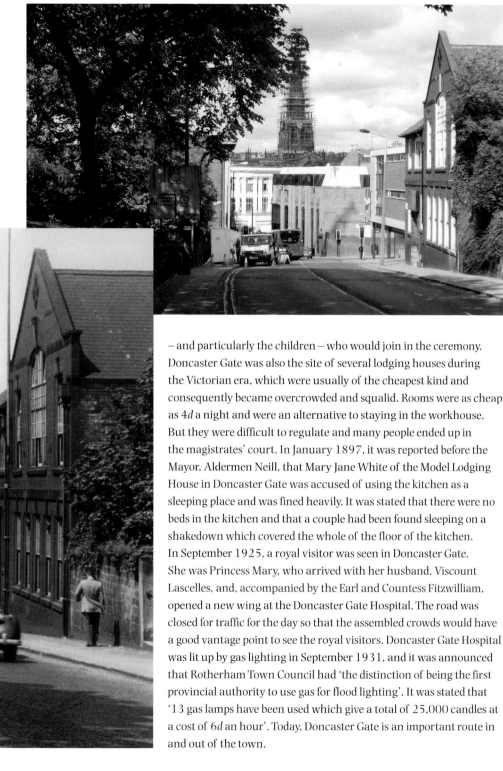

– and particularly the children – who would join in the ceremony. Doncaster Gate was also the site of several lodging houses during the Victorian era, which were usually of the cheapest kind and consequently became overcrowded and squalid. Rooms were as cheap as 4*d* a night and were an alternative to staying in the workhouse. But they were difficult to regulate and many people ended up in the magistrates' court. In January 1897, it was reported before the Mayor, Aldermen Neill, that Mary Jane White of the Model Lodging House in Doncaster Gate was accused of using the kitchen as a sleeping place and was fined heavily. It was stated that there were no beds in the kitchen and that a couple had been found sleeping on a shakedown which covered the whole of the floor of the kitchen. In September 1925, a royal visitor was seen in Doncaster Gate. She was Princess Mary, who arrived with her husband, Viscount Lascelles, and, accompanied by the Earl and Countess Fitzwilliam, opened a new wing at the Doncaster Gate Hospital. The road was closed for traffic for the day so that the assembled crowds would have a good vantage point to see the royal visitors. Doncaster Gate Hospital was lit up by gas lighting in September 1931, and it was announced that Rotherham Town Council had 'the distinction of being the first provincial authority to use gas for flood lighting'. It was stated that '13 gas lamps have been used which give a total of 25,000 candles at a cost of 6*d* an hour'. Today, Doncaster Gate is an important route in and out of the town.

EFFINGHAM SQUARE

THIS SQUARE, NAMED after the Earl of Effingham, was used for many different occasions in the town's history. Like the other squares in Rotherham, it was regularly used as a meeting place and also a place of entertainment. Throughout the 1850s, there were regular visits of Wombwell's Menagerie, which would be on show in the square. There were waxworks and ghost shows, Holden's marionettes, something described as 'Hamilton's Panorama', as well as other 'freaks

and monstrosities' on show. There was a merry-go-round, described as 'wooden horses driven by steam going round and round to the sound of a barrel organ'. It was also reported that, in front of the pavement by the Old Town Hall on Effingham Street, was a bazaar owned by Mr Donaldson, where parents could buy children's toys; there was also a collection of pie stalls, medicine stalls and singers. Around 1860, the square was host to the world-famous tightrope walker Blondin. Permission had been given to him to attach ropes from one side to the other, about 30ft from the ground. To make matters really interesting, he drove a man in a wheelbarrow across the rope to huge applause. Little remains of Effingham Square today, which is now pedestrianised, apart from the Effingham Arms public house. The pub was opened on 20 October 1860, and for its opening the landlord offered entertainment at his hotel. The celebrations consisted of a public dinner followed (strangely to our modern ears) by a 'grand concert of sacred music'. As well as professional singers, the host of the Effingham Arms contributed with a song of his own. This pub today thrives in the centre of the town.

EMPIRE CINEMA

BY DECEMBER 1913, the bottleneck at the top of the High Street had gone, making the road better for traffic. As part of the improvements, some properties were acquired by the Rotherham Corporation and sold off. Two local landlords, Mr Hafferty of the Ring O'Bells on Church Street, and Mr Steeples of the Grapes at Dalton Brook, got together to bring to Rotherham a theatre building which would be an ornament to the town. The theatre was intended to be part of a complex of shops attached to the building. These can clearly be seen in the photograph, which dates from shortly after the theatre opened on 15 December 1913, when it was described as:

...Absolutely amazing. A more delightful building could not be conceived and hearty congratulations are due to everyone concerned on the work that has been accomplished.

The theatre building was equipped with luxurious seating and lighting. There were two performances a day at 7 p.m. and 9 p.m. of 'a music hall variety consisting of shows, musical comedies, revues and pantomimes'.

The cost of the entrance fee was very low – from as little as 6*d*, 4*d* and 3*d*. People who required more expensive seats in the dress circle would pay just 1*s* and the theatre also boasted four elaborate private boxes. It was forecast that Shakespearian plays and operas would be performed there, as well as 'moving pictures'. The comic for the first week was a man named Arthur Roberts, who had been described as the 'Prince of Comedians'. The management assured its patrons that he was bringing to Rotherham the full cast of his London show. An orchestra had been engaged that would be conducted by a well-known Rotherham musician named Mr S. Burgan. On one occasion, the same orchestra played the 'Blue Danube' during a silent film on the same subject. It was reported by 'Vulcan' of the *Advertiser* in March 1974 that 'shows of almost three hours entertainment could be had for as little as a shilling'. He also reminisced that, 'when I think of the Empire I think of Fred Shaw', who managed the place for years with 'an attention to detail that put the Empire in a class of its own'. Unfortunately, today, the Empire looks rather shabby. Like many other old buildings in Rotherham, the Empire has now been converted into a nightclub.

FERHAM HOUSE

MANY PEOPLE HAVE lived in Ferham House since it was built by Jonathan Walker in 1787. We know that during the residency of a lawyer named William Fretwell Hoyle (1801–86), there were swans on the lake of the parkland which is now Ferham Park. This Grade II listed building has been the home of many of Rotherham's wealthier persons. We know that it was owned at some

time in 1878 by a Derby butcher called Mrs Simpson, who sold very cheap meat in a place called Simpson's Arcade, a former skating rink on Howard Street. There was much opposition to the cost of her meat by local butchers, and unfortunately Mrs Simpson went bankrupt just two years later in 1880. Another resident was the manager of the Midland Iron Works, a Mr George Charles Hague, who came to a sticky end in October 1871. It was reported that Mr Hague, aged fifty-six, had died at the Masbrough railway station. He was in the habit of crossing over the rail tracks to get to his iron works, and had been spotted doing so by the station master, Mr Herbert Thompson Brown, on many occasions. On the day in question, he had arrived at Masbrough from Chesterfield, and, whilst crossing the tracks, he fell – and before he could rise, a train ran over his legs. A tourniquet was applied and he was taken to Ferham House on a stretcher, where he later died of blood poisoning. At the inquest on his body, held at the Black Bull public house, the coroner and jury heard how the station master would rebuke others but, because of Mr Hague's position in society, nothing had been said to stop him from crossing the lines. He was buried at Wentworth on Thursday 5 October; he left a wife, a daughter and two sons. The house was opened as a child welfare clinic in 1920 to provide better healthcare for mothers and their babies. It was visited by Sir Neville Chamberlain in May 1927, who offered his congratulations to the town council for the great strides which had been made. Ferham House is now closed to the public and is run as a private nursing home.

FERHAM PARK

THE PARK WAS originally part of the grounds of Ferham House, but was bought by the Rotherham Council and opened for the public on Saturday, 25 June 1887. The town council wanted this to be more than a park for entertainment and it was known as the Masbrough Recreational Ground. Thousands of people gathered to attend the opening of the park, and a grandstand covered in bunting was erected to seat the dignitaries of the town. At right angles to this was a stand with seating for 600 children from Kimberworth School. The Rotherham Volunteers were assembled in a military parade attended by a brass band. The ceremony started with the band playing 'God Save the Queen', echoed by the children and the hundreds of people in the crowd. Revd W.H. Carr, the Vicar of Kimberworth, gave a short blessing. The Mayor, Alderman Wragg, announced that he was opening the park on behalf of the people of Kimberworth, Holmes and Masbrough. He told them that the intention was not for it to be a park in the conventional sense, but a place for exercise and sport. It was intended to have a path all the way round, which would be belted by trees. The centre of the grounds 'will remain grassed for the children to play cricket and other games on'. He told the people that they were not going to appoint a park keeper but that everyone would have that responsibility, as 'the park belonged to them'. The Volunteers, under Captain Hurst, sent a few volleys up into the air to even more cheering. The celebrations closed with a great show of fireworks in the evening, where another stand for 2,000 had been erected, including many of the inmates of the workhouse. The estimated crowds in attendance were said to be between 15,000 and 20,000. Today the park is still used for exercise, and a route which measures a quarter of a mile is regularly used by people of all nationalities. There is also a large area used for football, and a recently refurbished play park and skateboarding area. Perhaps if Alderman Wragg and the town council of 1887 were to look down on Ferham Park today, they would be pleased that their hopes for the park are being strictly adhered to.

HASTINGS CLOCK

E.L.S. 172-177. Coronation Fountain, Rotherham.

MANY PEOPLE ARE aware of the firm set up by James and William Hastings, which flourished in Bridgegate in the early part of the twentieth century. Less is known about the entrepreneurial efforts that the Hastings brothers made to establish their business. Their father, also called William, came to the area expecting to find the streets of Sheffield paved with gold. He was looking for a job as a silversmith, but instead established himself as a 'tally man', going door-to-door with goods on his back, collecting a weekly fee. His son James followed in his footsteps, and, at the age of twenty-six, bought a house in Effingham Street. He found that the house opposite was full of prostitutes, which would – even in those days – bring the value of his house down. James wrote to the owner of the property, not knowing that he had the full weight of the law on his side, and was surprised to learn that within four days the house was cleared. James's

brother William joined him in the business, and they noted that, on several occasions, they were asked for mangles or wringing machines by housewives whom they regularly visited. The brothers decided to buy some mangles on the understanding that they had to be displayed in the windows of the owners' houses. This strategy of relying on the one-up-manship of housewives ensured that the business became very successful, and the firm of James & William Hastings was born. On November 1911, in order to celebrate the Coronation of George V, James Hastings offered to present the town council with a handsome feature consisting of a clock, a drinking fountain and a horse trough. The Mayor, Mr P. Bancroft Coward, accepted the generous gift – which was erected the following year and placed in Effingham Square. Hastings told the Mayor that a miner had asked him if it was true that, for the first week, the drinking fountain would run with Mappin's beer – which gained him a round of applause. Mr Hastings told the Mayor that, as part of his work, he had travelled up and down Effingham Street for thirty years. During that time, the idea of a drinking fountain and horse trough had come to him. The clock, which has had several moves throughout the town, now stands in more or less the original situation in Effingham Square. The clock (which will soon celebrate its centenary) still overlooks the busy streets and keeps perfect time, although flowers now grow out of the horse trough. It is the timely reminder of the two brothers, who, through their ingenuity, brought a very successful store to Bridgegate.

HIGH HOUSE HOTEL

PUBLIC HOUSES ON the Crofts would have been a hive of activity during market days and would have done excellent business. It must have been a lucrative site, as there were several public houses here. To rival the hotel was the Black Swan, the Butcher's Arms, and the Cross Keys. By the 1850s, public houses opened at 5 a.m. or 6 a.m. and were open until 10.30 p.m., so it was a long day for busy landlords. The High House had been open for business since 1856, when the landlord was a man named Mr Charles Dobbs. Market days were frequently crowded, and people would come from miles around to buy refreshments from the public houses around the Crofts. Nevertheless, drunkenness was abhorred in the Victorian period.

Despite deterrents, more places selling alcohol were opening up. The Superintendent of Police, Major Hammond, stated in his annual report of 1887 that, 'there is in the district some 85 inns, 128 beer houses and ten other licensed houses totaling 223'. By 1958, regular inspections of public houses were undertaken to ensure a high standard was maintained. In a report of the licensing magistrates, concerning an inspection undertaken on 6 March, the High House was described as 'a good town house', but the owner, Frank Vernon Kavenagh, was criticized because 'one room urgently needs decorating'. Despite the proximity of the other public houses, trade was listed as being very good and his weekly sales amounted to '7 to 8 x 36 barrels and 50 dozen bottles of ale sold in a week'. Pubs like the High House provide relaxation for the people of the town through the provision of such games as cribbage and skittles. Large rooms were used for dances and there would be an atmosphere of music and singing, with the beer largely supplied by the local brewery, Mappin's or Bentley's. The High House is still in business today on the Crofts, with an outside seating area and excellent food.

HIGH STREET

THE HIGH STREET has always been the centre of the bustling heart of Rotherham. Taken in 1909, this photograph shows a prosperous street full of people busily shopping. However, the High Street has seen much misery and squalor. It is well known that a house on the High Street held Mary Queen of Scots, who stayed there as a prisoner on her journey from Bolton Castle in January 1569. Some historians say that it was the Crown Hotel, whilst others state it was in a house on the site of where the Old Bank now stands. The Feoffees, who were responsible for keeping her a prisoner, recorded the following payment: 'Item paid to Mr Lete for whacheng of ye Queene of Skottes 2/5d.' In *The Fiery Blades of Hallamshire: Sheffield and its Neighbourhood 1660–1740*, a letter is included showing correspondence between the Privy Seal, Sir F. Knollys and the Earl of Shrewsbury, who was responsible for conducting the royal prisoner to her

3293. HIGH STREET, ROTHERHAM.

destination. In the letter, the Earl notifies Sir Knollys of the illness of one of her ladies-in-waiting. He writes:

My ladie Leviston whom this Q doth exteme [esteem] most dearlye, did falle syche yesterdaye at Rotherham ymmediatelye before the said Q, coming away from thence.

The letter is subscribed 'In haste from Rotherham' and is dated 29 January 1569.

In the Victorian era, the High Street was noted as being an area where there was a lot of poverty. In 1886, such was the economic distress that when one of the workhouse guardians explored the area around the High Street, he found some 'truly chronic' cases needing food from the soup kitchen. It was not always the most sanitary street either. In October 1850, a complaint was made to the nuisance inspector about the dangerous and unsanitary condition of the High Street, which was thought to be caused by 'a stoppage at the main sewer'. The inspector ordered that the nuisance be cleared up without delay, but still complaints were heard. In June 1857, a letter was sent to the local newspaper complaining about the stench from the bottom of the High Street on Thursday night, 16 June, claiming that 'this wasn't the first time' that such complaints had been made. He stated that, 'if something is not done to put an end to this bother – especially in this hot weather – typhoid fever will be rampant in this place'. Thankfully, this type of problem has long since been eradicated. The High Street today cannot exactly be described as a bustle of activity and renewal, as many shops have closed down in recent years. But it still remains the heart of the town.

HOLLOWGATE

HOLLOWGATE IS TYPICAL of one of the main, although not very wide, entrances into the town. For many years, small packhorse trails would lead from Moorgate, down Hollowgate, and into Wellgate and the town centre. The area was visited by Celia Fiennes in 1697 when she travelled from Hemsworth to Rotherham. In her diary, entitled *Through Yorkshire on a Side Saddle in the Time of William and Mary: Being the Diary of Celia Fiennes* (featured in Herbert Wroe's *History of*

Rotherham) she wrote, 'thence to Rotherham 12 miles'. She described the journey as being 'mostly in a deep clay ground and now the ways are more difficult and narrow'. Smaller roads like Hollowgate would be damaged by timber carts being dragged by oxen as they travelled up and down the road. This would be further aggravated by damage inflicted by trailing sticks on wagons and carts, which were used as brakes on hills. Roads like Hollowgate would also be eroded by the weather, particularly on slopes, and they would literally become 'holloways' and thus named 'hollowgate', as in our present road. It was said that such roads were dusty to travel along in summer and became quagmires of mud in the winter. It was the responsibility of the town trustees to ensure that all the roads throughout the town were kept passable at all times. In 1735, Rotherham was prosecuted at the West Riding Quarter Sessions for its failure to repair its roads, as mentioned in Wroe's *History of Rotherham*. From about 1800, the population was no more than 4,000–5,000 people, and it was mainly an agricultural town, with houses clustered around the main streets of High Street, Westgate, Wellgate and Hollowgate, behind which existed fields and moorland. Blazeby tells us that when Robert Sanderson described entering Rotherham in the seventeenth century, he remembers seeing a 'pack of packhorses jingling bells from Wellgate along the narrow, rough road of Hollowgate to Whiston, Worksop and the London Road'. The photograph, taken in Wellgate in 1937, shows a row of mainly unoccupied dwelling houses. We can clearly see that the road has been vastly improved and widened from the hollowgate that it once was.

HOOD CROSS

AT THE JUNCTION of High Street, Doncaster Gate, College Street and Wellgate, a Hood Cross
was erected for the people of the town; it was a place around which to congregate and hear
proclamations and speakers. Bonfires were also set up here to celebrate public events. The records
of the Feoffees list that they erected the cross in 1595. It was recorded that year that they paid
Robert Banks 3s for 'leading the stone to ye crosse'. Another 18d was paid to John Pits for paving
the area around the cross, and a further payment was made to Edward Redwarde for setting up the
cross. Traditionally, Hood Crosses were also the place where open-air religious sermons would be
preached. By the eighteenth century, Methodism was becoming very popular and there were many

Rotherham Archives & Local Studies Service, photo 2330

non-conformist religious groups in the town. John Wesley held several meetings at the Hood Cross, where he preached sermons to working-class people. Herbert Wroe writes that when he preached for the first time, bonfires were lit at the site of the Hood Cross and at several other sites along Bridgegate, Millgate, High Street and Westgate. John Wesley came to Rotherham for the second time on 12 June 1755, when he recorded in his diary that there 'was such a number of people assembled as was never before seen in that town'. He came again on 25 July 1757 and 2 August 1759. The Hood Cross would also have been the place where proclamations were read out, keeping the people of Rotherham informed of what was happening on the wider world stage. Unfortunately, there is little evidence about how long the cross remained in place, but as carriages and carts became more evident, the cross would have had to be demolished at such a busy crossroads. We know also that during the First World War, and shortly after the sinking of the *Lusitania*, the place where the Hood Cross had stood for many centuries saw anti-German riots on 14 May 1915. The windows of shops belonging to citizens with German-sounding names were smashed and looting took place. Also at these crossroads, a boy was killed during the same riots by a lorry whose owner was found to be intoxicated. Today the area mainly exists as a busy junction, although parts of it have now been pedestrianised.

IMPERIAL BUILDINGS

THIS BEAUTIFUL GEORGIAN building was created when the town council decided that something had to be done about the bottleneck at the top of the High Street. Many of the buildings in the area were demolished in order to widen the road. One of these included the old Shambles Flesh Market, which was thought to have been built sometime in the 1800s. The market had little stalls where butchers sold meat and fishmongers sold fish, so, needless to say, the stench was unbearable. The layout of the Shambles consisted of twenty stalls around a central area and twenty-eight shops on the outside. The plan for the Imperial Buildings was to mirror the layout of the Shambles, in that there would be a series of shops placed around a central courtyard whilst the others

remained outside. The Imperial Buildings were designed by Mr Joseph Platts, at an agreed cost of £17,283. Sometime around 1905/6, the erection of the new Imperial Buildings began, finally being opened on Tuesday, 1 February 1908 by an ex-Mayor of Rotherham, Captain C.J. Stoddart. The plan for the opening ceremony was:

3.30 p.m.: The elected Mayor Councillor G H Lodge and Captain Stoddart along with other members of the council will assemble at the Town Hall.
3.45 p.m.: Invited guests will assemble at the Imperial Buildings.
3.45 p.m.: Members of the corporation, the Mayor and ex Mayor will walk to the Imperial Buildings via College Street and the High Street.
4.00 p.m.: The architect will present Captain Stoddart with the key to open the gateway to the building. The company will then pass through into the quadrangle of the building where there will be a short address.

The celebrations concluded with an afternoon tea served in a first-floor showroom situated at the corner of the High Street and Market Place. The tea was served to the civic dignitaries and their specially invited guests. Throughout the years, the building declined and, as recently as 2008, it was closed down for refurbishment. The building re-opened as a part of the All Saints Quarter, with a wide rang of popular shops and cafés, and remains as handsome today as it did when it first opened in 1908.

JOSEPHINE ROAD

DURING THE SECOND World War, many of the German bombs fell on the more industrial areas of Holmes and Masbrough due to their proximity to the railway lines. The damage which resulted from these raids is undetectable today, but the photo of some of the damaged houses on Josephine Road is an indication of what happened in the early hours of Thursday, 29 August 1940. Rotherham was very lucky and few people were killed during the air raids, unlike the nearby city

of Sheffield, where over 600 people lost their lives. Soon after the air-raid warning went off, the sound of aircraft could already be heard by the residents on Josephine Road, who took refuge in air-raid shelters and on cellar steps. Several of these aircraft were picked up by search lights, although many of them escaped into the clouds. Nothing is reported of the feelings of the people of Josephine Road on returning to their damaged houses. Incredibly, houses on the other side of the street were found to be barely damaged. Police and air-raid wardens, and other rescue parties, were already at work and they managed to save several uninjured persons who had been trapped under the debris. It was reported that one family had taken refuge on the cellar steps when a bomb struck the house. The explosion caused the door leading to the kitchen to be jammed, and also jammed the front door. The family had been forced to escape from the house by scrambling through a window. Thousands of panes of glass had been broken in houses and shops around Ferham Road and Josephine Road, and the pavements were littered with glass. Casualties were dealt with quickly, and wardens and police made immediate arrangements for the transport, accommodation and feeding for those made temporarily homeless. Demolition squads were at work soon after the air raid, dealing with property which had been made unsafe by the bombing. Despite the damage, the spirits of the people of Josephine Road were unbroken as they tried to return to some kind of normality. There is little doubt that the bravery of these people reflected the attitude of the population of Rotherham throughout the war years.

MASBROUGH EQUITABLE PIONEERS

ON 22 MARCH 1869, a group of traders started a co-operative which became known as the Masbrough Equitable Pioneers. They held their first meeting at the offices of the Midland Railway Company and, two days later, the first committee meeting of eight members was held in a private house on Princess Street, Masbrough, where the rules were drawn up. A month later, a shop was opened on Sarah Street, Masbrough and fitted up for business. Business expanded and, during the coming-of-age celebrations in April 1890, the treasurer stated that they now had departments for boots, drapery, clothing, coal, groceries and meat, plus a bake house and a penny bank. The last move that the Pioneers made was in April 1909, when they moved to Westgate. It was announced that the whole of the basement of the new premises was going to be used as a restaurant, and equipped with the latest cooking appliances. The floor was described as being a terrazzo pavement

and the walls had white-glazed bricks. A dinner to celebrate its opening took place on Wednesday 7 April. The entrance to the restaurant was in Domine Lane and the building was divided into three floors – one for furnishing and the other two for fish and game. The Pioneers' co-operative movement was very successful so there was great opposition in May 1925 when the decision was taken to change the name to the Rotherham Co-operative Society. But the Masbrough Equitable Pioneers' name was never removed from the building, and can still be seen at the top of the building today. Advertising was essential to any business, and an early advertisement announced at the beginning of the Second World War that, although they were unable to predict the outcome of the war:

We do know that we shall as always use our large buying power and extensive resources to maintain our stocks as complete as possible and to keep prices down to the lowest possible level. We shall not, by any present or future act of ours be found guilty of profiteering by the present uncertain conditions.

The opening hours of the showrooms which covered Westgate and Main Street were 7 a.m. until 9 p.m., and until 11 or 12 midnight on a Saturday. The only half days allowed for the hard-working shop staff were on Good Friday and Christmas Day. The Rotherham Co-operative Society successfully traded until the 1970s, when this photograph was taken. Unfortunately, today, as with many other buildings in the town, it is best known as the site of a nightclub.

MASBROUGH STATION

THIS BEAUTIFUL VICTORIAN station was opened in 1840 as part of the Manchester, Sheffield & Lincolnshire Railway, and became known as Midland Station or Masbrough Station. It has always been a popular site for the people of the town, and George Gummer tells us that huge crowds gathered here in 1876 when Charles Peace, who had been accused of murdering Arthur Dyson, was tried at Sheffield. On his way to the prison at Wakefield, hundreds of people assembled to catch a glimpse of him as he passed through Masbrough Station. The station was also a background for the departure of several Rotherham men accused of killing a gamekeeper. On Thursday, 16 November 1865, seven men accused of the murder of William Lilley were brought in chains to Masbrough Station in order to catch the 11.30 a.m. train to the Wakefield House of Correction. It would be hard to describe how the men felt, as they had all lived and poached in the area around Masbrough. William Sykes, one of the accused, had his daughter throw herself against him crying, knowing it was unlikely that she would ever see her father again. Later, they were convicted at York Assizes and transported out of England on the ship *Norwood* in April 1867, to spend the rest

of their lives in Western Australia. In March 1890, there was a collision at Masbrough Station and five passengers were injured when a Chesterfield to Sheffield train hit a goods vehicle. Thankfully, both trains were moving slowly but, inevitably, both lines up and down were blocked. Goods were scattered all over the lines, and one wagon was badly smashed and a second was derailed. The station master, Mr H.P. Jeffries, took immediate steps to help the injured, and two women, Mrs Vickers and her sister-in-law Mrs Eastwood, were taken to the nearby Prince of Wales Hotel to recover. Another injured passenger, Mrs Gilling, was sent to her home on College Road in a cab. Incredibly, the lines were cleared in less than an hour, when the station was once again open for business. In 1851, the railways were booming and the station at Masbrough ran several trains to London for people to visit the Crystal Palace. The return fare was advertised as only 5s, and the ticket allowed people to stay for as long as three weeks in the capital city. The scheme was most successful and thousands of Rotherham people took advantage of it. The station today is known as the Orient Express, an Indian restaurant serving a wide variety of authentic dishes; it is a popular venue for Asian weddings.

MASBROUGH STREET

ORIGINALLY, THE AREA around Masbrough was thought to have belonged to a man named 'Merc'. This notion is explored in John Guest's *Historic Notices of Rotherham*, in which it is suggested that 'Merc' built a fortification sometime in the sixth century, prior to the building of the town itself. The area around Masbrough remained very rural up to the 1850s, when it became more industrialised. On 4 May 1643, the Earl of Newcastle and his army of 8,000 men camped out on 'the fields where the township of Masbrough is now'. We also know that the fields around Masbrough were the first to be enclosed in 1765, to much opposition. Masbrough Street, which

runs through the heart of Masbrough, is the site of Millmoor Football Ground and the Millmoor public house. The Rotherham football team started around 1880 but, after several moves, the club decided on the Millmoor stadium. The first football match took place on 2 September 1907, when Rotherham County played Leeds City Reserves and won 3-2. Unfortunately, for the last few years, the grounds at Millmoor have been in a poor financial state and the stadium closed on 3 May 2008. At the last match held, Rotherham United won 1-0 against Barnet. The match was also attended by TV chef Jamie Oliver, who at that time was in Rotherham opening his shop, Ministry of Food. There may be a few Rotherham people who still remember the famous Tivoli Picture Theatre on Masbrough Street. The building, which had been run for many years by Messrs Henry Bray & Co., opened on Saturday, 5 April 1913. The theatre was described as one of the most 'comfortable, cosy and up-to-date picture theatres in the country'. Once 'talkies' were introduced, the theatre advertised as being equipped with the 'latest and best sound'. In September 1931, the Tivoli was advertising two of the latest films for the audiences of the town. On Monday, Tuesday and Wednesday they could see *War Nurse* with Robert Montgomery and Anita Page, which illustrated the 'woman's side of the Great War'. On Thursday, Friday and Saturday, citizens were entertained by Laurel and Hardy in *Another Fine Mess*. Today, nothing remains of the Tivoli buildings but an empty car park, which has remained unused since the closure of the Millmoor Football Ground.

MECHANICS' INSTITUTE AND ASSEMBLY ROOMS

THE NEED FOR a Mechanics' Institute to be established in the town had long been urged and, after a meeting at the courthouse on 31 August 1842, a committee was appointed to look into the matter. It took a while to find suitable premises, and the Institute opened on the corner of Howard Street and Effingham Street to a three-day celebration on 17, 18 and 19 October 1853. The ground floor held a lecture room, reading room, a library and two classrooms. On the second floor were a concert hall and an assembly room for the use of the people of the town. Also provided was a newsroom, which was stocked with London and provincial papers, including *Backwoods*, *Chambers*

Journal, Punch and the *Illustrated London News*. It was intended that the Institute would provide elementary and technical education for the working classes, but the same year it opened there were already complaints that 'the Mechanics Institute is mostly attended by persons of higher rank'. Annual subscriptions were dependent on the social status of its members. For example, people who were artisans or mechanics would pay a fee of 10*s* 6*d* a year, whilst businessmen would pay anything up to 2 guineas. For that they would have access to the library, the newsroom and the lecture rooms, which catered for 130 members. During the winter, lectures were heard and there were also instructions in mechanics, free-hand drawing and mathematics. By 1875–6, the Institute had approximately 200 members and the Earl of Effingham and Earl Fitzwilliam were its presidents. Many different temperance leagues would give lectures in the Assembly Rooms in the hope that they would keep young men out of the public houses. In February 1879, the Revd William Blazeby gave a lecture entitled 'An Evening with Oliver Goldsmith', which was described as 'a full and graphic account of the poet's life and writings, interspersed with excerpts from his poems'. In March 1880, performances by two sisters provided entertainment for the working-class men and women. The sisters, Sophie and Annie, entertained a 'respectable' audience with comic musical entertainment entitled 'Fun'. Several of the pieces were enthusiastically encored. The building was sold back to the council in 1892 and it was agreed that although there was no longer a need for a Mechanics' Institute, the first-floor concert rooms would continue as the Assembly Rooms. We know that some of the very earliest films were shown at the Assembly Rooms, until around 1911 when the first cinema opened in the town.

MOORGATE ROAD

ONE OF THE earliest routes into Rotherham led directly across Rotherham Moor, and for that reason became known as Moorgate Road. During the plague which hit Rotherham in 1589, temporary wooden huts were built on Moorgate for the victims, so they would be segregated from other townspeople. Strict watch was kept on those inflicted with the disease, until the infection ceased or they died and were buried. We see from the Feoffees' accounts that same year that 4*d* was paid 'to pore folk that ley on the more seke of the plague'. Entries for July show the plague at its height, and the Feoffees paid £100 for foodstuffs for the victims. Men were paid to watch the moors to ensure that no one entered or left the place, as we see in the two accounts:

Payd to Christofer Goodyeare for wardenge of the mours for 5 weeks   17s
Payd to Henry Fox for wardenge of ye more   7s

Later entries show that money had to be borrowed from the wealthier inhabitants of the town in order to meet the heavy expenditure for the Feoffees at this time. 10s was re-paid to Robert Oates the following year for money he had laid out during the plague time. It is also known from the Feoffees' accounts that Moorgate had a large wooded area, where pigs were kept which lived off acorns found in these woods; swineherds were paid to look after them. In 1617, a right of way was permitted 'across the more, down the Crofts and into the Hye Street'. Passage money amounting to 28s 6d was paid by the Feoffees to the Earl of Shrewsbury for this privilege. Revd Blazeby tells us that, on the Rotherham Moor, the people of the town assembled their arms, preparing to defend the town during the Civil War in September 1642. By 1786 Moorgate Road had become a turnpike road, where tolls had to be paid for admittance into the town; the tolls were used for the upkeep of the roads. During the Victorian era, prisoners could be dealt with summarily by magistrates at their own homes. Gummer talks about seeing prisoners in chains walking up Moorgate Road to the house of Mr Henry Jubb, a magistrate, in the company of police constables. Today there is no evidence of Moorgate's long journey through the history of the town. There are no woods and no swineherds. It is just a very pleasant road filled with some opulent detached houses.

OLD BANK

ON THE SITE where the Old Bank stands today, at the corner of High Street and Wellgate, there was once a mansion. It is supposed that Charles I spent the night in this mansion in Rotherham in 1647, when he escaped from the capital city and went to York. He fled in order to take up residence in the palace of the Archbishop. Following his surrender to the Scots, and on his way back to London, he was brought from Wakefield to Rotherham and thence to Mansfield. Blazeby tells us that there was a secret passage leading from the mansion, but its destination is not revealed. At some point, the mansion was demolished and we know that the original bank was founded in 1792 by three local families of the town named Walker, Eyre and Stanley, who also had a branch in Sheffield. It was one of the first banks to plough back profits and have a limited amount of banknotes issued. The bank was sold in 1836 and was renamed the Sheffield & Rotherham Joint Stock Banking Co. The *Business Directory of Sheffield* of 1862 lists the manager as being William Dyson. Gummer tells us that he lived on the premises and kept a very tight rein not only on the staff but on the customers also. The protocol of the bank demanded that male customers removed their hats as they entered, and pegs were provided for that purpose. Gummer also tells us that an earlier bank manager, Edward Heseltine (1828–53), was resident at the bank, where he managed to bring up a family of 'beautiful daughters'. It is also recorded that he complained to a Sanitary Enquiry held in 1850, claiming that half of the water closets of the High Street would drain into the bank's cellar, which required pumping out six or seven times a day. The Old Bank in the photograph was demolished in 1892 when the new 'Old Bank', now the Royal Bank of Scotland, was built.

OLD GRAMMAR SCHOOL

THE ORIGINAL ROTHERHAM Grammar School was established by Thomas de Rotherham around 1430, and was part of Jesus College. By 1547, the college had been disbanded; the school had moved to the half-timbered Town Hall and was now maintained by the Feoffees. By April 1857, the new schoolhouse was built at Moorgate at a cost of £1,300 for 100 boys. When it was discovered that the paths and boundaries still needed to be finished off, there was a major panic to make sure that the school was finished in time for the official opening on 4 June. The Grammar School had earned a name for excellence, as several boys were entered for Oxford and Cambridge examinations. However,

there was much indignation against the headmaster, Mr J.J. Christie, who, in 1868, attacked a boy who had killed his pet jackdaw. The case was brought to court by irate parents but it was thrown out by the magistrates. A letter defending Mr Christie was sent to the local newspaper on 19 December 1868. The letter, written from someone signing themselves as 'Fair Play', stated that the boy had tortured the jackdaw before killing it and, when Mr Christie had gone to admonish the boy, he had refused to assume the position to be caned. Mr Christie followed him and caned him severely; the attack was witnessed by the other boys. 'Fair Play' stated that the jackdaw incident could not have been ignored by the headmaster, and he had been forced to take action 'to show the other boys that such things could not be done at his school with impunity'. Despite the fact that the case led to an uproar in the town, confidence was shown in the headmaster, who was still in the post seven years later. It was recorded that, every year, the Feoffees granted eight free scholarships to the poorer boys of the town, the holders of which had a red tassel on their mortar boards. Fee-paying scholars had black tassels on theirs. Gummer states that these hats made formidable weapons, as the square corners were capped with tin and were used in schoolboy fights. The building on Moorgate was to accommodate the schoolroom and the headmaster's house. In the large schoolroom, several classes were accommodated and must have been incredibly noisy. The college lasted until 1889, when larger premises were found further up Moorgate in a building that was formerly the Rotherham Independent Theological College. The premises had been put up for sale and the Vicar of Rotherham suggested to the Feoffees that it would be ideal for the new Grammar School. It was bought at a knock-down price of £8,800. The more recent photograph shows that the building (which still stands) has now lost the large tower.

OLD MARKET

THERE HAVE BEEN several market places within the town throughout the years. Although it is unclear where the first market was held, it would most likely have been in a central part of the town. We know that within this early market place was the Town Hall, which was a half-timbered frame building, and nearby were the town stocks. It was thought that the original stocks were placed there around 1592. It is recorded in the Feoffees' accounts that, on 19 May 1611, a man,

one John Ralphe, escaped from the stocks and, as a consequence, had to be brought back from Whiston at a cost of 3*d*. In 1780, the stocks and the pillory were removed from the market place and taken to the church steps.

In the late eighteenth century, the market was on the site of the Shambles. It is said that the stall holders of the market ensured that it was the centre of gossip and scandal. Gummer talks about the open market and the noisy stall holders shouting out their wares. There were stalls selling vegetables, boots and shoes, hosiery, prints, earthenware and oilcloths, jostling shoulder-to-shoulder with vendors of quack medicine and sellers of all kinds of drinks. A newer market was built in 1879; however, it only lasted nine years before being destroyed by fire on Saturday, 21 January 1888. The fire was discovered by stall holders closing up at 11 p.m. when it was found that, incredibly, there was no water in the building. The water works manager had to be roused from his bed to turn on the water at the mains before the fire could be fought. By then the market was almost completely wrecked and the damage was estimated at being over £10,000. Too late, the Corporation found out that the insurance on the building had been minimal. The only part left was a triple gable end; this was incorporated into the new building on the same spot, which was opened on 18 December 1889. By 1972, the market was becoming rather shabby and it was decided that a new market would be built in the town centre. The Centenary Market now has an inside and outside market, and a variety of stalls selling goods of all descriptions.

OLD TOWN HALL

THE OLD TOWN Hall started its life as a block of buildings which included a savings bank and several offices. The whole site had been bought by the council in 1895 in order to allow for expansion of civic offices. From its position on Effingham Street, it was the site of many of the local celebrations held in the town. Herbert Wroe tells us of a great procession which took place on 5 November 1788 to commemorate the centenary of the 'Glorious Revolution', which was the replacement of King James II by William of Orange. A ball had been held at the Town Hall on the previous evening, and a dinner was given later in the day which was presided over by the Earl of Effingham. The celebrations were described as 'having rounds of cannons during the day and fireworks at night'. Further celebrations were recorded in June 1923, when all the streets in the vicinity of the Town Hall were decorated for the visit of the Prince of Wales, the future Duke of Windsor. The local newspaper records that when his open Crossley car drove around the corner of Effingham Street, there was a tremendous cheer from the crowd as they waved flags. As he descended from his car, the order to 'present arms' was given to the 5th Battalion of the York and Lancaster Regiment. He was greeted by the Mayor, resplendent in his scarlet robes and chain of office. The Prince was introduced to the Mayor by the Earl of Effingham. Three cheers were given by the crowd and then there was a shout of 'one for his father', which was 'responded to with zest'. After inspecting the Guard of Honour, the Prince entered the Town Hall – the entrance of which had been converted into a reception room for the occasion. Settees and comfortable chairs had been provided by the local firm of James & William Hastings. It was reported that 'the Prince appeared nervous as he frequently clutched at his tie and coat sleeves'; nevertheless, the royal visit was long remembered by the people of the town. Mayoral duties are many and varied, and it caused some surprise in March 1938, during a town council meeting, when the Mayor, Councillor Fowler, read out a letter from a 'Shy Jack Tar'. The letter announced that the writer was a Rotherham man serving with the Royal Navy at Malta, and he was looking for a 'nice young lady' from Rotherham as a pen pal. The Mayor said he was happy to help the young man and asked that all applications from local girls be sent to him at the Mayor's Parlour. The building remained as a Town Hall until 1988, when it was converted into a shopping complex and remains as such today.

POST OFFICE

THE OLD POST office was originally situated in the High Street, in premises near to the entrance of Three Cranes Yard. In 1750, it was recorded that the post office was run from the Angel Hotel on the High Street. William Wilson was recorded not only as being the licensee but also a seller of books, stationery and newspapers. At the weekends, it was his habit to read the news out from the newspapers to his patrons. In 1853, Joseph Roger Owen became the post master and, when he died in 1873, his wife (who continued the business) was known as 'Widow Owen'. The building was also used as a postal address for discreet young women looking for employment, as we see in an advertisement in the local papers for 1861, which contained an appeal:

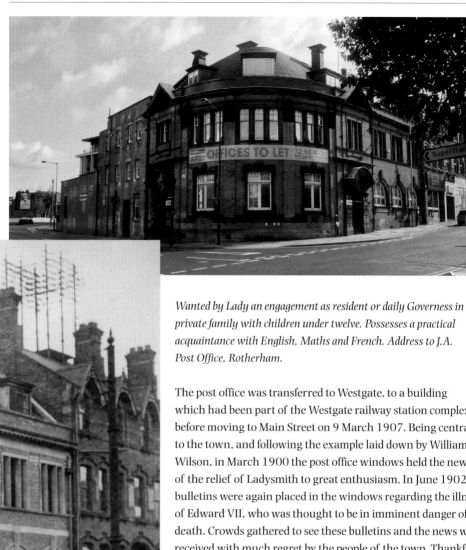

Wanted by Lady an engagement as resident or daily Governess in private family with children under twelve. Possesses a practical acquaintance with English, Maths and French. Address to J.A. Post Office, Rotherham.

The post office was transferred to Westgate, to a building which had been part of the Westgate railway station complex before moving to Main Street on 9 March 1907. Being central to the town, and following the example laid down by William Wilson, in March 1900 the post office windows held the news of the relief of Ladysmith to great enthusiasm. In June 1902, bulletins were again placed in the windows regarding the illness of Edward VII, who was thought to be in imminent danger of death. Crowds gathered to see these bulletins and the news was received with much regret by the people of the town. Thankfully, Edward recovered and was crowned in August. In both World Wars, war bonds were sold at the post office in order for the government to be able to pay the money it was costing to keep the war going. A sorting office was opened on Masbrough Street, near to the football ground, in order to relieve space at the main post office and, as early as 1956, there were plans to move to a new post office headquarters at the Central railway station across the road on Main Street. In December 1985, a decision was made that the old post office would close and a new post office would open in the new Cascades Shopping Centre in the town. The following August, the post office opened on Bridgegate, and still survives today.

PREMIER PICTURE PALACE

AS WE HAVE seen, between the years of 1908 and 1913 there were many theatres opening in the town. One which was dedicated solely for films was the Premier Picture Palace on Kimberworth Road. This cinema opened its doors for the first time on 9 December 1912, and was said to be one of the most modern and up-to-date in the town. Films were to be changed twice a week, on Monday and Thursday, and prices ranged from 1*d* to 6*d*. Situated conveniently for the many houses around Holmes, Masbrough, Kimberworth and Ferham, the cinema could hold over 1,000 people. During silent films, it was said that the Premier Picture Palace had many very versatile

pianists, who managed to show great dexterity in matching the mood of the films on the screen. When 'talkies' were introduced in July 1931, the Premier opened with the film *Whoopee*, starring Eddie Cantor, which was based on the Ziegfeld Broadway production. The film, which was typical of the era, was described as 'an all dancing, all singing production' and was very popular in its time. These films attracted mass audiences and, throughout the 1930s and '40s, the Premier saw people of the town indulging in the cheap entertainment that cinema provided. But what kind of films were the cinema audiences watching? By September 1940, one of the favourite films on show at the Premier was *These Glamour Girls*, starring Lew Ayres and Lana Turner. The film was supported by the 'Singing Cowboy', otherwise known as Gene Autry in *Home on the Prairie*. The following Thursday, the main film was one of the Andy Hardy films made popular by Mickey Rooney. Like many cinemas of the period, the introduction of television dealt a death blow to picture houses. Films were rapidly falling out of fashion and bingo was introduced by July 1961. At first, it was just on Sundays, and then gradually the week was split into two, with four days of bingo and films being shown the rest of the week. With the decline of the cinema, full-time bingo sessions started in October 1961, with the exception of the Saturday matinee for young children. Proving once again its adaptability to the demands of the public, on 5 December 1984, the Premier Picture Palace became a snooker hall and still exists today as such.

PSALTERS LANE

FOR CENTURIES, THE majority of travellers used ancient trackways into the town, and many of these pathways still survive today. These routes would have been used by pedlars and dealers in all kinds of comestibles, and, for hundreds of years, the principal import was salt. For this reason, the roads would have been called salt or salters routes. Salt was a commodity which was very necessary, as it was used for preserving food as well as for taste. Salt was a precious mineral which existed from very early days; in fact, in the Bible, Jesus praised someone by calling them 'the salt

of the earth'. It was said that Roman soldiers were paid in salt and that's where the expression 'worth his salt' comes from. Indeed, it was so valuable that many of these packhorse groups would combine for safety, earning the name 'salt trains'. These would consist of a number of mules or donkeys, carrying panniers filled with salt. David Hey suggests that it was not until the eighteenth century that the P was added – in the mistaken belief that the route through Rotherham was associated with the monks of Beauchief Abbey. Psalters Lane in Rotherham extends from Wortley Road, down through Kimberworth and Masbrough, and into the town centre. Other routes leading out of the town extended to Doncaster, the ports of Gainsborough, Barnsley and Sheffield. As a remembrance of this trade, many public houses and inns along the route were named after the 'packhorse', such as the Packhorse Inn on Doncaster Gate. These ancient routes form the basis of our modern roads. Such roads were levelled and paved, and houses were built up around them, forming the nucleus of the town that we know today. Psalters Lane today shows no indication of its ancient history, but it is undoubtedly one of the oldest roads into the town. Salt, as a commodity, has now lost its value, but we can still see its legacy in these ancient trackways.

REGAL THEATRE

THE REGAL THEATRE on Corporation Street was opened on Saturday, 22 December 1934, by local comedian Sandy Powell and the Deputy Mayor, Alderman Kirk. Sandy Powell, who had been born in Rotherham in 1900, told Alderman Kirk that he was delighted to be back in his hometown and was thrilled to be asked to open the Regal Theatre. The local newspapers reported that:

> For many months there had been incredible interest in the swarms of builders, decorators, architects and electricians that have been working on the site for 21 weeks. A sense of ease and well being settles on patrons passing through the door into the beautiful foyer behind.

The first film to be shown in the theatre, starting at 7.30 p.m., was *Girls, Please!* starring Sydney Howard, a Yorkshire film star. A unique feature offered by the managers of the Regal were the ten-minute organ recitals which were given during the interval, played by Thomas Dando. Dando

had been heard on the 'wireless' on many occasions, and was greatly missed when he left Rotherham a few years later. In 1974, 'Vulcan' of the *Advertiser* stated that the Conacher organ on which Dando gave his recitals would then be worth £80,000, as it was the only organ of its kind in the world. During the war, in January 1941, the Regal was showing *Gasbags*, starring the Crazy Gang, which was very popular. No doubt desperate to smile during the privations of the war, the audience laughed throughout the film. At the end of the war, and in a change to its more secular pursuits, the Regal Theatre was the only place large enough to hold a thanksgiving service for the five battalions of the Home Guard. The ceremony, which took place in December 1944, was attended by a crowd of almost 2,000 people and was solemnised by the Bishop of Sheffield and the Vicar of Rotherham. The cinema later showed the May 1945 VE celebrations, in a change to the usual programme of Hollywood movies. The film showed the service of thanksgiving, the praise given to the hundreds of munitions workers by civic dignitaries, as well as some of the street parties which had been held. A later manager was a man called Fred Morris, who was responsible for historic newsreels of Rotherham United, a team that he followed faithfully. These weekly sports films attracted large audiences. Today, the Regal has changed its name to Mecca Bingo and is frequented by the hundreds of bingo aficionados of the town.

ROTHERHAM MINSTER

THE MINSTER STARTED life as All Saints' parish church and is thought to be five centuries old. Built on the site of the original Saxon church, there is evidence that the early church had a strong door which could be barred, in order that people fleeing from arrest could claim sanctuary. The *Ivanhoe Review* tells us that some remains of a large door jamb, and some adjoining strong walls, were found under the north-west pier of the church during some alterations. Following the Reformation in 1536, when churches were stripped of anything regarded as 'popish', the Rotherham churchwarden accounts show that a payment of *3d* was made to Robert Bate and Thomas Dawson, for 'helping to take down the hye aulter stone and other things' from All Saints' Church. A further payment of *3s 2d* was made for 'taking down the tabernaykyle'. But the churchgoers, who

were notoriously non-conformist in Rotherham, made up their own rules. Most people of England were opposed to the introduction of the Book of Common Prayer in 1549, imposed by Henry VIII's son Edward VI. However, David Hey states that, in Rotherham, there was such haste to conform under young Edward that the town churchwardens paid for handwritten copies of the prayer book until such time as printed copies were available. The churchyard surrounding the Minster contains many graves. Revd Blazeby reports that, in 1780, a giant of a man known as John Cutforthay, who was a surgeon and a wine merchant of Rotherham, died and was buried at the church. He was aged sixty-five and was estimated to be 6ft 3in tall, and around 40 stone in weight. At the funeral, his coffin was said to be so broad that three men could comfortably lay down in it side by side. The only way that he could have been lowered into the ground was by the use of pulleys. We know that the church's misfortunes include being set on fire in the 1820s, when some men who had been working on the roof left a fire on the leads. Whilst they were at lunch, the lead began to melt, and molten metal ran down into the church, setting the pews on fire. Bad luck continued when the church was struck by lightning in June 1880.

I find it strangely moving that, after the death of Queen Victoria had been announced on Saturday, 2 February 1901, there was a spontaneous gathering of thousands of Rotherham people at the Minster. The people wanted to pay their last respects to the monarch who had been on the throne for over sixty years. In an unplanned symbol of patriotism, it was said that nearly 2,000 people were packed into the Minster. The Minster today continues to hold the long tradition of providing services for the people of the town.

THOMAS ROTHERHAM COLLEGE

THE BUILDING THAT became Thomas Rotherham College was built in 1876 as a theologian college and cost £26,000. However, after only twelve years it was agreed that the college would merge with the Airedale College at Bradford, and the building was put up for sale. As we have seen, it later became the new Grammar School and was officially opened by the Archbishop of York on 8 May 1890. The building was described by John Guest as a 'fine battlemented and turreted college'. The school was ahead of its time and had a laboratory, built in 1890, equipped with twenty-four benches, a lecture room and a workshop; a gym was added later. The Grammar School had an 'old boys association' by 1925, and many of them attended the unveiling of a memorial to those old boys who had been killed in the war. The ceremony, which took place on Thursday, 19 February, was held by Revd Hargreaves Heap, and the memorial was unveiled by the

Archbishop of York. On the tablet were fifty-eight names, all of which were read out by the headmaster. The Grammar School was given its new name of the Thomas Rotherham College in 1966. The college received a financial boost in August 1980, when it was found that a painting which had been donated a few years earlier by Mr Arthur Badger was worth £4,800. The picture, of a Norman knight, was painted by Richard Beavis, and was discovered when an art historian went to the college to advise on the restoration of some of the other pictures. In 1997, the college received an outstanding set of grades, which put it in the top ten nationally. The college certainly lives up to its mission statement, which is 'to provide a high quality learning experience' for both staff and pupils.

WELLGATE

WELLGATE IS THOUGHT to have acquired its name due to the wells which supplied water to much of the town. We know that a stream of water flowed down Wellgate and continued down Bridgegate and into the river. The origin of the street goes back to 1490. According to *Victorian Rotherham* by Tony Mumford, a man called Thomas Webster bequeathed 3*s* 4*d* for the making of a street called 'Welgate'. Also, in a charter of 1427–8, it was referred to as the 'street of the rivulets'. It was recorded in *The Feoffees of the Common Lands of Rotherham: A Brief Historical Sketch* that a rivulet rose 'at Broome Valley which runs through the bottom end of Gerard Road and then underground to a point about 30 yards below Mansfield Road where it became a stream'. Along Wellgate were two other wells, named Tinkers Well and Bishops Well. Gummer tells us that there

were two pumps situated on Wellgate, one near the Mail Coach Inn and the other about 20 yards beyond Mansfield Road on the right-hand side. The stream was covered over about 1791–2. The supply was so good that people came to collect water from other areas. In a book about reminiscences of Rotherham, one person remembers:

About 5 a.m. on most Sundays there would be about 50 men carrying two buckets in order to fill them and carry them back to Masbrough where there was little water apart from what was got out of the canal or the River Don. It was also common for youths to be involved in carrying water to Masbrough before washing day, which was undertaken in several homes.

The Wellgate water must have had some quality, as it was also known around the town that Countess Fitzwilliam regularly sent servants to collect some of the water for her tea. If Her Ladyship ventured into the town to do some shopping, she would carry two stone jars, which would be filled and put in her carriage to take home to the estate of Wentworth Woodhouse. What people would probably like to forget about Wellgate is that there was a fascist headquarters there – to which a group returned on 13 September 1934 following an attack on some communists on St Ann's Road. It has to be said that fascism was not tolerated in Rotherham – although Oswald Mosley's visit the following year was (uncharacteristically for Rotherham) reported to be a 'quiet meeting'. Although many shops have been closed nearer to the town centre in the modern photograph, Wellgate remains today an area filled with shops and public houses which cater to every need.

WEST RIDING COURTHOUSE/TOWN HALL

THE FIRST WEST Riding Courthouse was opened on College Square on Monday, 6 January 1826. There had been many demands for a courthouse and, such was the desperate need, that, after the stone-laying ceremony on 11 September 1826, a 'grand dinner' was given for magistrates and officials. The courthouse had been built by the Feoffees at a cost of £5,000, and was described as having ample accommodation for the Quarter and Petty Sessions. Adjoining it was a house for the Superintendent of Police, and the building included ten good prison cells. Roughly 100 years later, the second West Riding Courthouse was deemed necessary. A suitable building was built on the

Crofts and opened on 6 May 1929. Built of Portland stone, the ground floor contained offices for police. The entrance on Moorgate Street led into a large parade room and the cells for the prisoners. Upstairs were the retiring rooms for magistrates and their clerks, as well as two large courtrooms and waiting rooms for witnesses. The public entrance, which is on the Crofts, gave access to the public galleries via a central staircase. The very first case that was heard in the new courtroom was that of an eighteen-year-old colliery pony driver, who was sentenced to six months' imprisonment for stealing £5 10s. He was also charged with breaking and entering a shop, and stealing 3s and a quantity of cigarettes. When his room was searched, police found the money under his mattress. The court was told that he was already on two years' probation and his father refused to be in court with him. The magistrate informed him that if he had been younger he would have been sent to Borstal. Sentencing him, the magistrate stated a hope that he would 'come out a better lad', and it was reported that several women in the gallery began to cry. A new police station was opened on Main Street in October 1982, but, almost as soon as it opened, there was criticism about the danger posed by the transportation of high-risk prisoners from the police station to the magistrates' court on the Crofts. Finally, permission was given in February 1987 for a new magistrates' court to be built on Main Street, on the site of the old 'stattis' (statute) fairground, which would cost over £3 million. The former West Riding Courthouse received a major renovation before opening as the new Town Hall. Just recently, the building has once more been updated and enhanced at a cost of £2.9 million. There are now more meeting rooms, the Mayoral Suite has been refurbished, and provision has been made for couples who wish to get married in this beautiful building.

WHITE HART HOTEL

THE RE HAS BEEN a White Hart Hotel building in the Church Street area since 1739. The building was so central to the town that it was reported that a night watchman had a sentry box outside it in the 1830s. The box was situated next to the front door of the building; another box was situated on Westgate next to the Wellington Inn. The original White Hart Hotel had played an important part in the business life of Rotherham during the nineteenth century. For many years, it was a flourishing meeting place on market days because of its excellent stabling facilities. It also played a part as the headquarters of the Yorkshire Dragoons when Earl Fitzwilliam was their captain. According to George Gummer, the building was reputed to be the 'trysting place of many of the town's notable characters and gossips' and was christened Westminster for that very reason. The upper-class drinkers of the town would be entertained on the top floor of the hotel, which became known as

the 'House of Lords', and the middle-class imbibers would be found on the first floor, known as the 'House of Commons'. The original White Hart was against the wall of the churchyard, but was demolished in 1929 when All Saints Square was formed. When the new building was opened in December 1929, the local newspaper stated that 'its transformation has been nothing short of remarkable'. The new building belonged to Messrs Mappin of the Old Brewery at Masbrough, and added into it were valuable shops, offices and bank buildings. The new White Hart faces Church Street and there was once an entrance from Bridgegate, although I am not sure if it is still in use. The accommodation at the newly refurbished hotel was reported as including:

A new lounge, smoke room, luncheon room and a bar parlour. There is a large club room capable of seating up to 80 guests but which can also be divided by screens and ample bedrooms with bathrooms for guests. Situated at the corner of the new hotel is a shop with a store underneath. The building holds no less than sixteen first floor and second floor offices which can be accessed by a staircase and an electric lift.

The sign of the White Hart, which can be seen on the top of the pictured building, was repeated on the lead work, stained glasswork and in the plaster of the interior. At its position in the centre of the town, the imposing façade today is used as a solicitor's office.

BIBLIOGRAPHY

Primary Source Material

Feoffees' accounts
County Borough of Rotherham: Report of the Licensing Magistrates, 1958–59
Commercial Directory for 1814–15 (Wardle and Bentham Publishers)
Slater's Directory of Yorkshire (1848)
Business Directory of Sheffield (J.S.C. Morris, 1862)
Baines, W., *Directory of Yorkshire* (1822)

Secondary Source Material

Books
Blazeby, Revd W., *Rotherham Old Meeting House* (H. Garnett & Co., 1906)
Cator, P.M., *So Great a Cloud of Witnesses: A History of the People of All Saints Church Rotherham 1483–1983* (Rotherham Library and Information Service, 1983)
Coburn, J.H., *Rotherham Lawyers* (Henry Garnett & Co. Ltd., 1932)
Guest, J., *Historic Notices of Rotherham* (Robert White, 1879)
Guest, J., *Relics and Records* (Rotherham Metropolitan Public Library, 1865)
Gummer, G., *Reminiscences of Rotherham and District* (Garnetts & Co., 1927)
Hey, D., *The Fiery Blades of Hallamshire: Sheffield and its Neighbourhood 1660–1740* (Leicester University Press, 1991)
Hill, N., *Postal History of Rotherham* (1960)
Mumford, A., *Victorian Rotherham* (Quoin Publishing Ltd, 1989)
Reminiscences of Rotherham (Henry Garnett, 1891)
Satterthwaite, P., *Rotherham Town Public Houses 1820–1990* (Rotherham Public Library, 1991)
Smith, H., *The History of Rotherham Roads and Transport* (Rotherham Metropolitan Borough Council, 1992)
Smith, S., *Movie Palaces of Rotherham* (Rotherham Metropolitan Borough Council, 1993)
The Feoffees of the Common Lands of Rotherham: A Brief Historical Sketch (Garnett, 1978)
Worrall, J.R., *A Brief History of Boston Castle and Parklands* (Friends of Boston Castle and Parklands, undated)
Wroe, H., *History of Rotherham* (unpublished manuscript, c. 1930)

Articles
'The Unsatisfactory State of Rotherham Town Centre and Associated Housing Conditions in 1897' in *Ivanhoe Review*, Vol. I, No. 2, November 1899

Newspapers
The Rotherham and Masbrough Advertiser